Artist
Bob Bampton

Cover
Jim Channell

Acknowledgements

ARDEA, London: 8U (D Burgess); 11B (L & T Bomford); 12U (W Weisser); 14U (B Bevan); 15U (I Beames); 21B (F Gohier); 22BL (A Warren); 27U (J-P Ferrero); 29B (W Moller). **BRUCE COLEMAN**: title page (D & M Plage). **FRANK LANE**: 9U (Silvestris/Frank Lane); 16U (S McCutcheon): 18U (W Wisniewski): 22U (Silvestris/Frank Lane); 25U (F Hartmann). **NHPA**: 11U (A Bannister); 19B (ANT/NHPA); 23U (E H Rao); 24U (E A James). **OXFORD SCIENTIFIC**: 26B (J A L Cooke); 30B (G I Bernard). **SURVIVAL ANGLIA**: 9C (C Buxton/A Price); 18 inset (A Root); 21U (J & D Bartlett); 22BR (J Foott).

ISBN 0 86112 434 0

Published by Brimax Books, Newmarket, England 1987
Printed in Belgium
Second printing 1987.

ANIMAL LIFE
Growing Up

Written by
Karen O'Callaghan &
Kate Londesborough

BRIMAX BOOKS • NEWMARKET • ENGLAND

Contents

Baby animals

The world is a new and very strange place for all baby animals.

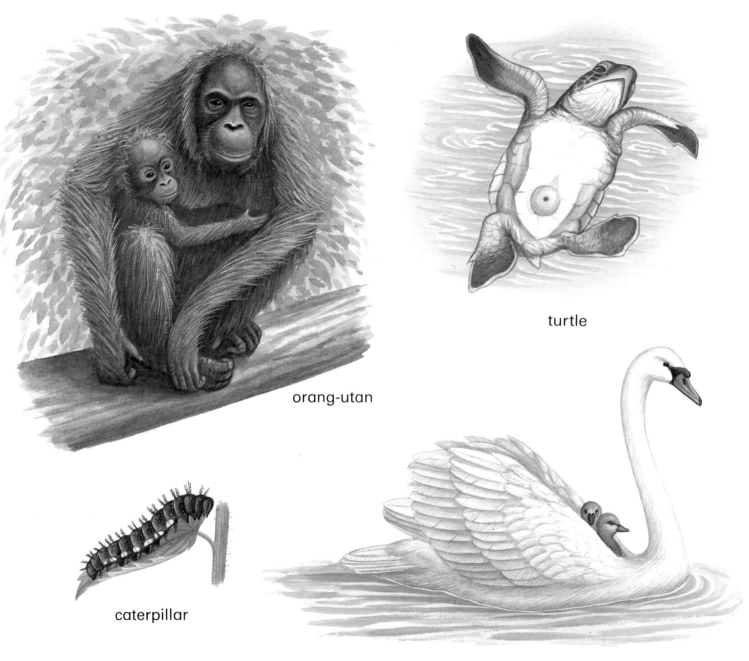

turtle

orang-utan

caterpillar

swans

Some stay with their parents. Others live alone and take care of themselves. They all have a lot to learn.

Born all alone

These babies can all look after themselves as soon as they are born. Their parents do not stay with them.

Before they hatch, **snakes** grow an egg tooth. They use this sharp tooth to cut open the shell. These baby snakes will find their own food.

egg tooth

The baby **dog shark** has a yolk-sac joined to its body. The newborn shark feeds on this.

Mother **turtles** lay their eggs in the sand and leave them.

Soon the babies dig their way out and rush into the sea. This is a dangerous time for the baby **turtles**. Some of them are eaten by birds before they reach the water.

This **monarch butterfly** lays her eggs on a leaf.

The **caterpillars** will eat the leaf as soon as they are born.

Cared for at birth

When these babies are born, their parents feed them and protect them from danger.

Baby **shrews** are born in a nest made of dry grasses. When they are strong enough to leave the nest, the family all stay together.

When they are born, **kittens** have their eyes closed. After one week their eyes will open. The kittens stay close to their mother and suck her milk. They cannot look after themselves. The mother cat licks their fur to clean them.

10

The baby **hippopotamus** is born under the water. It learns to swim alongside its mother. It will be able to swim before it learns to walk on land. These babies live in special nursery groups with other mothers and babies.

Cichlids (*siklids*) carry their young in their mouths. They let them out to feed. If an enemy comes too close, they suck the babies in again.

Weak and strong

Some babies are born weak and helpless.
They stay with their parents for many weeks.
They need a safe home while they grow.

Song sparrows are born in a nest in the grass. At first they are blind. They have no feathers and cannot stand up or walk. Their parents bring them food.

The **macaque** does not build a nest for her baby. She keeps it warm and safe in her arms. At first, the baby is so weak that it can only cling to her and suck milk. After many weeks it will be strong enough to ride on her back.

The mother **dog** knows her puppies will be safe by her side. If one wanders away, she carries it back by the scruff of its neck.

Squirrels make a nest of sticks for their babies. They will stay in the nest for 8 weeks. If there is danger, the mother squirrel will move her babies to a safer place.

Other babies still need care, but are much stronger when they are born.

Mallard ducks use their nest only for a short time. When the ducklings hatch they can see and they have soft feathers. As soon as the feathers dry, they all leave the nest for water. The ducklings can swim and their mother shows them where to find their own food.

Baby **hares**, called leverets, are born with fur and their eyes are open. They can run about after only a few minutes. They drink milk from their mother at first, but will soon find small plants to eat by themselves.

The mother **reindeer** does not build a nest. Her calf is born on to the ground. The herd must keep moving to find food. After resting for two days the calf will be able to walk with them.

The young **bush-baby** is born covered with hair. After one day it can run quite fast along the branches. It sucks its mother's milk and after two weeks it will also eat soft fruit.

Where are they born?

In a tunnel

A **platypus** lays two eggs in a tunnel. At first, the babies are naked and blind.

In a fur-lined nest at the end of a tunnel these baby **rabbits** are born. They grow quickly. At two weeks old they can run.

In a cave

Polar bear cubs are
born deep in
a snow cave.
At birth they are very small, only 25 cms (10 inches) long,
and they are blind and deaf. They will not be able to hear
for nearly 3 months.

Under a tree

The **tiger** cubs are
hidden under
a fallen tree. When
they are born, they
are blind and very
tiny.

In a pouch

size at birth

A baby **red kangaroo** is as long as a thumb nail when it is born. It is called a joey. It lives in its mother's pouch and will climb back in even when it has grown much bigger.

Virginia opossums have 13 tiny babies. They stay in the pouch for 10 weeks. Then they are carried about by their mother.

18

In a tree

Sloths live high up in the trees. The baby is born upside-down and holds on to its mother's fur.

On the ice

Emperor penguins live in the snow and ice. The chick hatches during the winter. The father holds it on a fold or flap of skin, resting on his feet. This keeps the chick warm.

In the water

A baby **blue whale** is born under the water. It is born tail first so that it will not drown. As soon as its head is out, its mother nudges it up to the air to breathe. Another female swims nearby, watching out for sharks.

On the ground

Zebras are born on the open plains. After one hour
the foal struggles to its feet and walks with the herd.
Its legs are wobbly. It sucks milk for 10 days
and then starts to eat grass.

On a rock

This baby **seal** is
born on the open
rock. After a rest,
mother and baby
will swim together
in the open sea.

How many babies?

An **elephant** has one baby.

An **ostrich** lays up to 15 eggs.

The **armadillo** has four babies. They are identical quads.

A **tiger** can have one, two, three or four cubs.

A **Nile crocodile** can lay up to 95 eggs.

This **toad** lays up to 20,000 eggs.

A **mosquito** lays up to 300 eggs.

A **cod** lays 5 million eggs.

Family life

Some babies are looked after by their mother and father.

These baby **swans**, called cygnets *(signets)*, are protected from their enemies. If the cygnets are in danger, the swans will fight with their wings and beaks.

Coyote pups live in a den built by their parents. When they are newly born, the father hunts for the whole family.

Other animals live in larger groups where families live together.

When she has a baby, the mother **elephant** is helped by other females. They all help to protect the elephant calf.

Two **badger** families live in this underground home. It is called a set. The parents make a little room for the cubs. Soon all the badgers will play together.

Caring mothers

Most baby animals are cared for by their mothers.

The mother **crocodile** guards her eggs until they hatch. When they are born, she takes them to a quiet pool in her mouth.

Baby **scorpions** are carried on their mother's back. She protects them with her poisonous sting.

The baby **orang-utan** is very small and weak when it is born. The mother carries it all the time for the first few months.

Caring fathers

In some families the father works hard to look after the young.

The mother **seahorse** lays her eggs in a pouch on the father's belly. He cares for the eggs. Five weeks later he releases nearly one hundred babies.

The male **Darwin frog** keeps the eggs safe in his mouth. They stay there until they are tiny frogs. Then he opens his mouth and the little frogs jump out.

The male **stickleback** builds a nest of weeds. The female lays her eggs inside and swims away. The father then guards the nest and he will look after the babies when they hatch.

Strange families

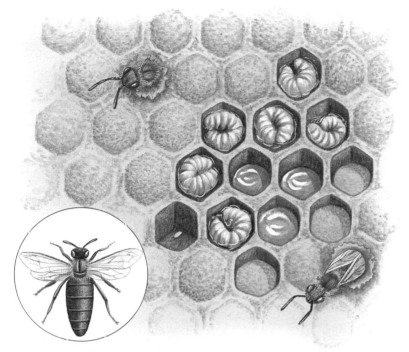

queen bee

These young **bees** all have the same mother. She is the queen bee. Her only job is to lay eggs.

Cuckoos lay their eggs in other birds' nests. The new foster parents will feed and look after the baby cuckoo as if it was their own.

The **spiny anteater** lays one egg. She grows a pouch to keep the egg warm. When the baby grows, it sucks milk from inside the pouch. The pouch will close when the baby no longer needs it.

When they are born these **greenfly** have tiny little eggs inside them. In eight to ten days each greenfly has its own babies. The mother can give birth to 25 babies every day.

Playing and learning

Baby animals learn by playing with each other and watching the older animals.

Chimpanzees play chase in the trees. The babies run and dodge. They learn how to escape from their enemies.

Otters need to catch fish for food. Baby otters must learn to swim fast. They like playing games, making slides and splashing each other.

Bear cubs roll over each other and pretend to fight. This makes them strong. They see the adult bears having real fights.

Some parents teach the young animals how to hunt and find food.

The mother **leopard** teaches her cub to hunt in the forest. It learns to move quietly and to lie in wait ready to pounce on a passing animal.

The **fox** teaches its cubs to hunt. Cubs must learn to run fast and pounce at the right moment. This adult has some food in his mouth. He holds it just out of reach and runs away. The cubs try to take the food.

Young **beavers** watch their parents find food. They learn which plants are good to eat.

Growing and changing

Some babies do not look like their parents.

Frog

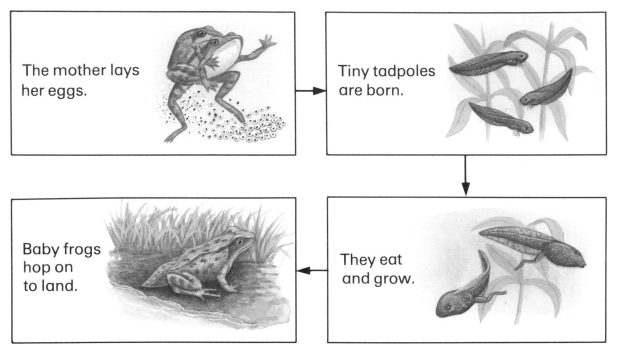

The mother lays her eggs.

Tiny tadpoles are born.

They eat and grow.

Baby frogs hop on to land.

Butterfly

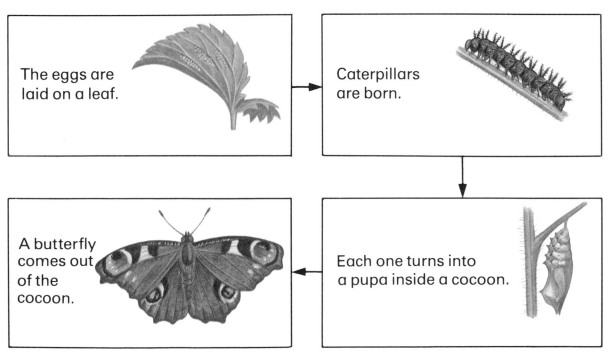

The eggs are laid on a leaf.

Caterpillars are born.

Each one turns into a pupa inside a cocoon.

A butterfly comes out of the cocoon.

These babies look like their parents.

Cricket

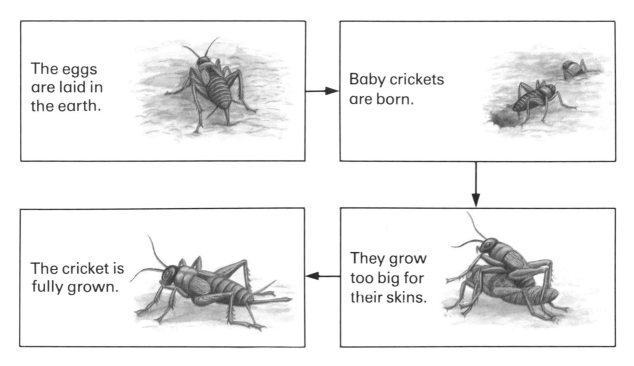

The eggs are laid in the earth.

Baby crickets are born.

They grow too big for their skins.

The cricket is fully grown.

Lion

The female cub looks like her mother. The male cub will have a long mane when he grows up.

female

male

Growing up

Some babies grow up quickly, others grow slowly. It is a long time before they become adult and can have babies of their own.

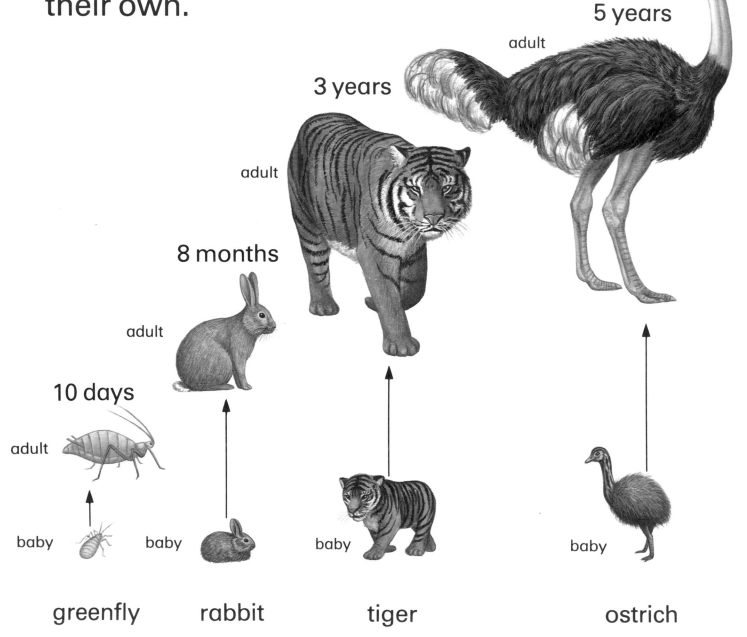

5 years
adult

3 years

adult

8 months

adult

10 days

adult

baby

baby

baby

baby

greenfly

rabbit

tiger

ostrich

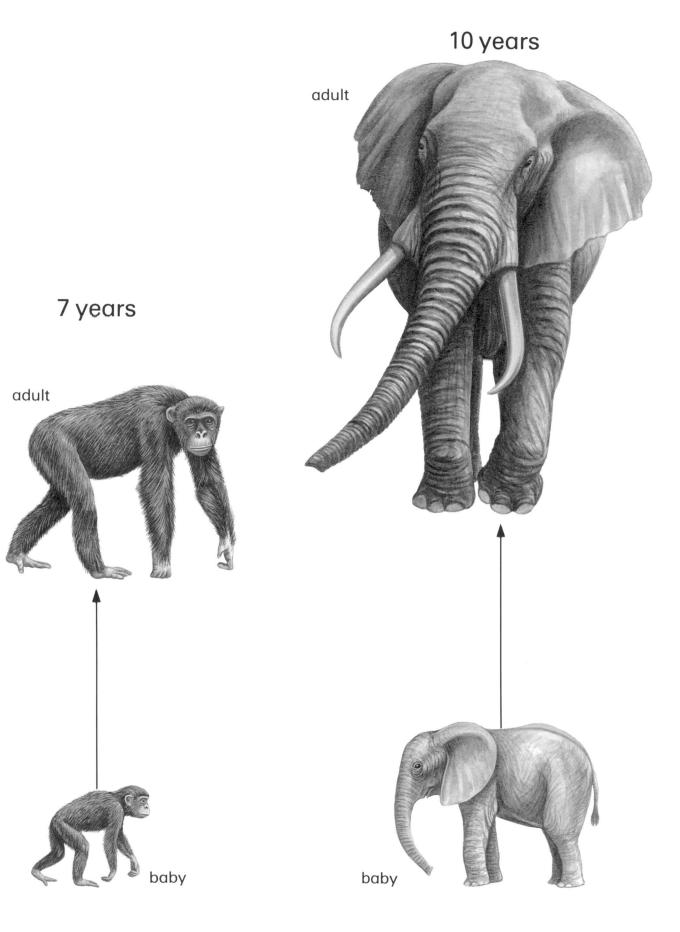

10 years

adult

7 years

adult

baby

baby

chimpanzee

elephant

Index